Ocean Animals

# Sea Horses

by Christina Leaf

BELLWETHER MEDIA
MINNEAPOLIS, MN

**Blastoff! Beginners** are developed by literacy experts and educators to meet the needs of early readers. These engaging informational texts support young children as they begin reading about their world. Through simple language and high frequency words paired with crisp, colorful photos, Blastoff! Beginners launch young readers into the universe of independent reading.

Blastoff! Universe ★

Reading Level — Grade K

Grades 1-3

Grade 4

## Sight Words in This Book 🔍

| | | | |
|---|---|---|---|
| are | have | not | they |
| can | in | of | to |
| do | it | one | water |
| eat | long | the | well |
| find | many | there | you |

This edition first published in 2021 by Bellwether Media, Inc.

No part of this publication may be reproduced in whole or in part without written permission of the publisher. For information regarding permission, write to Bellwether Media, Inc., Attention: Permissions Department, 6012 Blue Circle Drive, Minnetonka, MN 55343.

Library of Congress Cataloging-in-Publication Data

Names: Leaf, Christina, author.
Title: Sea horses / by Christina Leaf.
Description: Minneapolis, MN : Bellwether Media, 2021. | Series: Blastoff! beginners: ocean animals | Includes bibliographical references and index. | Audience: Ages PreK-2 | Audience: Grades K-1
Identifiers: LCCN 2020031984 (print) | LCCN 2020031985 (ebook) | ISBN 9781644873960 (library binding) | ISBN 9781648340734 (ebook)
Subjects: LCSH: Sea horses--Juvenile literature.
Classification: LCC QL638.S9 L434 2021 (print) | LCC QL638.S9 (ebook) | DDC 597/.6798--dc23
LC record available at https://lccn.loc.gov/2020031984
LC ebook record available at https://lccn.loc.gov/2020031985

Text copyright © 2021 by Bellwether Media, Inc. BLASTOFF! BEGINNERS and associated logos are trademarks and/or registered trademarks of Bellwether Media, Inc.

Editor: Amy McDonald    Designer: Andrea Schneider

Printed in the United States of America, North Mankato, MN.

# Table of Contents

# Sea Horses!

Sea horses
are not horses!
They are fish!

Sea horses live
in **shallow** water.
There are
many kinds
of sea horses.

common
sea horse

pygmy sea horse

spiny sea horse

# Body Parts

Sea horses have curved bodies.

Sea horses have long **snouts**. They suck in food.

snout

Sea horses
have curled tails.
They hold plants.

plants

tail

Sea horses
have small **fins**.

fin

# The Lives of Sea Horses

Sea horses
eat tiny animals.
Shrimp are
the best!

shrimp

Sea horses stay
in one place.
They do not
swim well.

Sea horses
change color
to hide.
Can you find it?

# Sea Horse Facts

## Sea Horse Body Parts

snout

fin

tail

curved body

## Sea Horse Food

shrimp

small fish

plankton

# Glossary

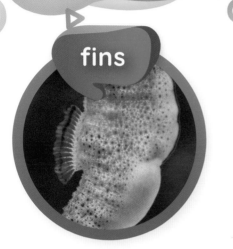

thin body parts
that stick out

**shallow**

not deep

**snouts**

noses and mouths

# To Learn More

## ON THE WEB

## FACTSURFER

Factsurfer.com gives you a safe, fun way to find more information.

1. Go to www.factsurfer.com.

2. Enter "sea horses" into the search box and click 🔍.

3. Select your book cover to see a list of related content.

## Index

The images in this book are reproduced through the courtesy of: imagebroker.com/ SeaTops/ Ardea, front cover; Eric Isselee, pp. 3, 10 (snout); rognar, pp. 4-5; Frolova_Elena, p. 6; WhitcombeRD, pp. 6-7; Levent Konuk, p. 7 (pygmy); Daniel Lamborn, p. 7 (spiny); Kristina Vackova, pp. 8-9; SergeUWPhoto, pp. 10-11; Kichigin, p. 12; semet, pp. 12-13; frantic00, pp. 14-15; Napat, pp. 16 (shrimp), 22 (plankton); scubadesign, pp. 16-17; Akos Kreicz, pp. 18-19, 23 (snouts); DiveSpin.Com, pp. 20-21; Dennis van de Water, p. 22 (parts)l Rattiya Thongdumhyu, p. 22 (shrimp); Choksawatdikorn, p. 22 (small fish); Ivalin, p. 23 (fins); stockphoto-graf, p. 23 (shallow).